MW00879620

Glenn & Sue Hawks
119 Don Felipe Way
Ojai, Calif 93023

The Majesty of Calmness

Individual Problems and Possibilities

by

William George Jordan

Author of "The Kingship of Self-Control"

Originally published: 1900

CONTENTS

I

The Majesty of Calmness

Calmness is the rarest quality in human life. It is the poise of a great nature, in harmony with itself and its ideals. It is the moral atmosphere of a life self-centred, self-reliant, and self-controlled. Calmness is singleness of purpose, absolute confidence, and conscious power,--ready to be focused in an instant to meet any crisis.

The Sphinx is not a true type of calmness,--petrifaction is not calmness; it is death, the silencing of all the energies; while no one lives his life more fully, more intensely and more consciously than the man who is calm.

The Fatalist is not calm. He is the coward slave of his environment, hopelessly surrendering to his present condition, recklessly indifferent to his future. He accepts his life as a rudderless ship, drifting on the ocean of time. He has no compass, no chart, no known port to which he is sailing. His self-confessed inferiority to all nature is shown in his existence of constant surrender. It is not,--calmness.

The man who is calm has his course in life clearly marked on his chart. His hand is ever on the helm. Storm, fog, night, tempest, danger, hidden reefs,--he is ever prepared and ready for them. He is made calm and serene by the realization that in these crises of his voyage he needs a clear mind and a cool head; that he has naught to do but to do each

day the best he can by the light he has; that he will
never flinch nor falter for a moment; that, though he
may have to tack and leave his course for a time, he
will never drift, he will get back into the true
channel, he will keep ever headed toward his
harbor. *When* he will reach it, *how* he will reach it,
matters not to him. He rests in calmness, knowing
he has done his best. If his best seem to be
overthrown or overruled, then he must still bow his
head,--in calmness. To no man is permitted to know
the future of his life, the finality. God commits to
man ever only new beginnings, new wisdom, and
new days to use the best of his knowledge.

Calmness comes ever from within. It is the peace
and restfulness of the depths of our nature. The fury
of storm and of wind agitate only the surface of the
sea; they can penetrate only two or three hundred
feet,-- below that is the calm, unruffled deep. To be
ready for the great crises of life we must learn
serenity in our daily living. Calmness is the crown
of self-control.

When the worries and cares of the day fret you, and
begin to wear upon you, and you chafe under the
friction,--be calm. Stop, rest for a moment, and let
calmness and peace assert themselves. If you let
these irritating outside influences get the better of
you, you are confessing your inferiority to them, by
permitting them to dominate you. Study the
disturbing elements, each by itself, bring all the will
power of your nature to bear upon them, and you
will find that they will, one by one, melt into
nothingness, like vapors fading before the sun. The
glow of calmness that will then pervade your mind,

the tingling sensation of an inflow of new strength, may be to you the beginning of the revelation of the supreme calmness that is possible for you. Then, in some great hour of your life, when you stand face to face with some awful trial, when the structure of your ambition and life-work crumbles in a moment, you will be brave. You can then fold your arms calmly, look out undismayed and undaunted upon the ashes of your hope, upon the wreck of what you have faithfully built, and with brave heart and unfaltering voice you may say: "So let it be,--I will build again."

When the tongue of malice and slander, the persecution of inferiority, tempts you for just a moment to retaliate, when for an instant you forget yourself so far as to hunger for revenge,--be calm. When the grey heron is pursued by its enemy, the eagle, it does not run to escape; it remains calm, takes a dignified stand, and waits quietly, facing the enemy unmoved. With the terrific force with which the eagle makes its attack, the boasted king of birds is often impaled and run through on the quiet, lance-like bill of the heron. The means that man takes to kill another's character becomes suicide of his own.

No man in the world ever attempted to wrong another without being injured in return,--someway, somehow, sometime. The only weapon of offence that Nature seems to recognize is the boomerang. Nature keeps her books admirably; she puts down every item, she closes all accounts finally, but she does not always balance them at the end of the month. To the man who is calm, revenge is so far beneath him that he cannot reach it,--even by stooping. When injured, he does not retaliate; he wraps around him the royal robes of Calmness, and he goes quietly on his way.

When the hand of Death touches the one we hold dearest, paralyzes our energy, and eclipses the sun of our life, the calmness that has been accumulating in long years becomes in a moment our refuge, our reserve strength.

The most subtle of all temptations is the *seeming* success of the wicked. It requires moral courage to see, without flinching, material prosperity coming to men who are dishonest; to see politicians rise into prominence, power and wealth by trickery and corruption; to see virtue in rags and vice in velvets; to see ignorance at a premium, and knowledge at a discount. To the man who is really calm these puzzles of life do not appeal. He is living his life as best he can; he is not worrying about the problems of justice, whose solution must be left to Omniscience to solve.

When man has developed the spirit of Calmness until it becomes so absolutely part of him that his very presence radiates it, he has made great progress in lite. Calmness cannot be acquired of itself and by itself; it must come as the culmination of a series of virtues. What the world needs and what individuals need is a higher standard of living, a great realizing sense of the privilege and dignity of life, a higher and nobler conception of individuality.

With this great sense of calmness permeating an individual, man becomes able to retire more into himself, away from the noise, the confusion and strife of the world, which come to his ears only as faint, far-off rumblings, or as the tumult of the life of a city heard only as a buzzing hum by the man in a balloon.

The man who is calm does not selfishly isolate himself from the world, for he is intensely interested in all that concerns the welfare of humanity. His calmness is but a Holy of Holies into which he can retire *from* the world to get strength to live *in* the world. He realizes that the full glory of individuality, the crowning of his self-control is,-- the majesty of calmness.

II

Hurry, the Scourge of America

The first sermon in the world was preached at the Creation. It was a Divine protest against Hurry. It was a Divine object lesson of perfect law, perfect plan, perfect order, perfect method. Six days of work carefully planned, scheduled and completed were followed by,--rest. Whether we accept the story as literal or as figurative, as the account of successive days or of ages comprising millions of years, matters little if we but learn the lesson.

Nature is very un-American. Nature never hurries.

Every phase of her working shows plan, calmness, reliability, and the absence of hurry. Hurry always implies lack of definite method, confusion, impatience of slow growth. The Tower of Babel, the world's first skyscraper, was a failure because of hurry. The workers mistook their arrogant ambition for inspiration. They had too many builders,--and no architect. They thought to make up the lack of a head by a superfluity of hands. This is a characteristic of Hurry. It seeks ever to make energy a substitute for a clearly defined plan,--the result is ever as hopeless as trying to transform a hobby-horse into a real steed by brisk riding.

Hurry is a counterfeit of haste. Haste has an ideal, a distinct aim to be realized by the quickest, direct methods. Haste has a single compass upon which it relies for direction and in harmony with which its course is determined. Hurry says: "I must move faster. I will get three compasses; I will have them different; I will be guided by all of them. One of them will probably be right." Hurry never realizes that slow, careful foundation work is the quickest in the end.

Hurry has ruined more Americans than has any other word in the vocabulary of life. It is the scourge of America; and is both a cause and a result of our high-pressure civilization. Hurry adroitly assumes so many masquerades of disguise that its identity is not always recognized.

Hurry always pays the highest price for everything, and, usually the goods are not delivered. In the race for wealth men often sacrifice time, energy, health, home, happiness and honor,--everything that money cannot buy, the very things that money can never bring back. Hurry is a phantom of paradoxes. Business men, in their desire to provide for the future happiness of their family, often sacrifice the present happiness of wife and children on the altar of Hurry. They forget that their place in the home should be something greater than being merely "the man that pays the bills;" they expect consideration and thoughtfulness that they are not giving.

We hear too much of a wife's duties to a husband and too little of the other side of the question. "The wife," they tell us, "should meet her husband with a smile and a kiss, should tactfully watch his moods and be ever sweetness and sunshine." Why this continual swinging of the censer of devotion to the man of business? Why should a woman have to look up with timid glance at the face of her husband, to "size up his mood"? Has not her day, too, been one of care, and responsibility, and watchfulness? Has not mother-love been working over perplexing problems and worries of home and of the training of the children that wifely love may make her seek to solve in secret? Is man, then, the weaker sex that he must be pampered and treated as tenderly as a boil trying to keep from contact with the world?

In their hurry to attain some ambition, to gratify the dream of a life, men often throw honor, truth, and generosity to the winds. Politicians dare to stand by and see a city poisoned with foul water until they "see where they come in" on a water-works appropriation. If it be necessary to poison an army,-

-that, too, is but an incident in the hurry for wealth.

This is the Age of the Hothouse. The element of natural growth is pushed to one side and the hothouse and the force-pump are substituted. Nature looks on tolerantly as she says: "So far you may go, but no farther, my foolish children."

The educational system of to-day is a monumental institution dedicated to Hurry. The children are forced to go through a series of studies that sweep the circle of all human wisdom. They are given everything that the ambitious ignorance of the age can force into their minds; they are taught everything but the essentials,--how to use their senses and how to think. Their minds become congested by a great mass of undigested facts, and still the cruel, barbarous forcing goes on. You watch it until it seems you cannot stand it a moment longer, and you instinctively put out your hand and say: "Stop! This modern slaughter of the Innocents must *not* go on!" Education smiles suavely, waves her hand complacently toward her thousands of knowledge-prisons over the country, and says: "Who are you that dares speak a word against our sacred, school system?" Education is in a hurry. Because she fails in fifteen years to do what half the time should accomplish by better methods, she should not be too boastful. Incompetence is not always a reason for pride. And they hurry the children into a hundred textbooks, then into ill-health, then into the colleges, then into a diploma, then into life,--with a dazed mind, untrained and unfitted for the real duties of living.

Hurry is the deathblow to calmness, to dignity, to poise. The old-time courtesy went out when the new-time hurry came in. Hurry is the father of dyspepsia. In the rush of our national life, the bolting of food has become a national vice. The words "Quick Lunches" might properly be placed on thousands of headstones in our cemeteries. Man forgets that he is the only animal that dines; the others merely feed. Why does he abrogate his right to dine and go to the end of the line with the mere feeders? His self-respecting stomach rebels, and expresses its indignation by indigestion. Then man has to go through life with a little bottle of pepsin tablets in his vest-pocket. He is but another victim to this craze for speed. Hurry means the breakdown of the nerves. It is the royal road to nervous prostration.

Everything that is great in life is the product of slow growth; the newer, and greater, and higher, and nobler the work, the slower is its growth, the surer is its lasting success. Mushrooms attain their full power in a night; oaks require decades. A fad lives its life in a few weeks; a philosophy lives through generations and centuries. If you are sure you are right, do not let the voice of the world, or of friends, or of family swerve you for a moment from your purpose. Accept slow growth if it must be slow, and know the results *must* come, as you would accept the long, lonely hours of the night,--with absolute assurance that the heavy-leaded moments *must* bring the morning.

Let us as individuals banish the word "Hurry" from our lives. Let us care for nothing so much that we would pay honor and self-respect as the price of hurrying it. Let us cultivate calmness, restfulness, poise, sweetness,--doing our best, bearing all things as bravely as we can; living our life undisturbed by the prosperity of the wicked or the malice of the envious. Let us not be impatient, chafing at delay, fretting over failure, wearying over results, and weakening under opposition. Let us ever turn our face toward the future with confidence and trust, with the calmness of a life in harmony with itself, true to its ideals, and slowly and constantly progressing toward their realization.

Let us see that cowardly word Hurry in all its most degenerating phases, let us see that it ever kills truth, loyalty, thoroughness; and let us determine that, day by day, we will seek more and more to substitute for it the calmness and repose of a true life, nobly lived.

III

The Power of Personal Influence

The only responsibility that a man cannot evade in this life is the one he thinks of least,--his personal influence. Man's conscious influence, when he is on dress-parade, when he is posing to impress those around him,--is woefully small. But his unconscious influence, the silent, subtle radiation of his personality, the effect of his words and acts, the trifles he never considers,--is tremendous. Every moment of life he is changing to a degree the life of the whole world. Every man has an atmosphere which is affecting every other. So silent and unconsciously is this influence working, that man may forget that it exists.

All the forces of Nature,--heat, light, electricity and gravitation,-- are silent and invisible. We never *see* them; we only know that they exist by seeing the effects they produce. In all Nature the wonders of the "seen" are dwarfed into insignificance when compared with the majesty and glory of the "unseen." The great sun itself does not supply enough heat and light to sustain animal and vegetable life on the earth. We are dependent for nearly half of our light and heat upon the stars, and the greater part of this supply of life-giving energy comes from *invisible* stars, millions of miles from the earth. In a thousand ways Nature constantly seeks to lead men to a keener and deeper realization of the power and the wonder of the invisible.

Into the hands of every individual is given a marvellous power for good or for evil,--the silent, unconscious, unseen influence of his life. This is simply the constant radiation of what a man really *is*, not what he pretends to be. Every man, by his mere living, is radiating sympathy, or sorrow, or morbidness, or cynicism, or happiness, or hope, or any of a hundred other qualities. Life is a state of constant radiation and absorption; to exist is to radiate; to exist is to be the recipient of radiations.

There are men and women whose presence seems to radiate sunshine, cheer and optimism. You feel calmed and rested and restored in a moment to a new and stronger faith in humanity. There are others who focus in an instant all your latent distrust, morbidness and rebellion against life. Without knowing why, you chafe and fret in their presence. You lose your bearings on life and its problems. Your moral compass is disturbed and unsatisfactory. It is made untrue in an instant, as the magnetic needle of a ship is deflected when it passes near great mountains of iron ore.

There are men who float down the stream of life like icebergs,--cold, reserved, unapproachable and self-contained. In their presence you involuntarily draw your wraps closer around you, as you wonder who left the door open. These refrigerated human beings have a most depressing influence on all those who fall under the spell of their radiated chilliness. But there are other natures, warm, helpful, genial, who are like the Gulf Stream, following their own course, flowing undaunted and undismayed in the ocean of colder waters. Their presence brings warmth and life and the glow of sunshine, the joyous, stimulating breath of spring. There are men who are like malarious swamps,-- poisonous, depressing and weakening by their very presence. They make heavy, oppressive and gloomy the atmosphere of their own homes; the sound of the children's play is stilled, the ripples of laughter are frozen by their presence. They go through life as if each day were a new big funeral, and they were always chief mourners. There are other men who seem like the ocean; they are constantly bracing, stimulating, giving new draughts of tonic life and strength by their very presence.

There are men who are insincere in heart, and that insincerity is radiated by their presence. They have a wondrous interest in your welfare,--when they need you. They put on a "property" smile so suddenly, when it serves their purpose, that it seems the smile must be connected with some electric button concealed in their clothes. Their voice has a simulated cordiality that long training may have made almost natural. But they never play their part absolutely true, the mask *will* slip down sometimes; their cleverness cannot teach their eyes the look of sterling honesty; they may deceive some people, but they cannot deceive all. There is a subtle power of revelation which makes us say: "Well, I cannot explain how it is, but I know that man is not honest."

Man cannot escape for one moment from this radiation of his character, this constantly weakening or strengthening of others. He cannot evade the responsibility by saying it is an unconscious influence. He can *select* the qualities that he will permit to be radiated. He can cultivate sweetness, calmness, trust, generosity, truth, justice, loyalty, nobility,--make them vitally active in his character,--and by these qualities he will constantly affect the world.

Discouragement often comes to honest souls trying to live the best they can, in the thought that they are doing so little good in the world. Trifles unnoted by us may be links in the chain of some great purpose.

In 1797, William Godwin wrote The Inquirer, a collection of revolutionary essays on morals and politics. This book influenced Thomas Malthus to write his Essay on Population, published in 1798. Malthus' book suggested to Charles Darwin a point of view upon which he devoted many years of his life, resulting, in 1859, in the publication of The Origin of Species,--the most influential book of the nineteenth century, a book that has revolutionized all science. These were but three links of influence extending over sixty years. It might be possible to trace this genealogy of influence back from Godwin, through generation and generation, to the word or act of some shepherd in early Britain, watching his flock upon the hills, living his quiet life, and dying with the thought that he had done nothing to help the world.

Men and women have duties to others,--and duties to themselves. In justice to ourselves we should refuse to live in an atmosphere that keeps us from living our best. If the fault be in us, we should master it. If it be the personal influence of others that, like a noxious vapor, kills our best impulses, we should remove from that influence,-- if we can *possibly* move without forsaking duties. If it be wrong to move, then we should take strong doses of moral quinine to counteract the malaria of influence. It is not what those around us *do* for us that counts,--it is what they *are* to us. We carry our house- plants from one window to another to give them the proper heat, light, air and moisture. Should we not be at least as careful of ourselves?

To make our influence felt we must live our faith,

we must practice what we believe. A magnet does not attract iron, as iron. It must first convert the iron into another magnet before it can attract it. It is useless for a parent to try to teach gentleness to her children when she herself is cross and irritable. The child who is told to be truthful and who hears a parent lie cleverly to escape some little social unpleasantness is not going to cling very zealously to truth. The parent's words say "don't lie," the influence of the parent's life says "do lie."

No man can ever isolate himself to evade this constant power of influence, as no single corpuscle can rebel and escape from the general course of the blood. No individual is so insignificant as to be without influence. The changes in our varying moods are all recorded in the delicate barometers of the lives of others. We should ever let our influence filter through human love and sympathy. We should not be merely an influence,--we should be an inspiration. By our very presence we should be a tower of strength to the hungering human souls around us.

IV

The Dignity of Self-Reliance

Self-confidence, without self-reliance, is as useless as a cooking recipe,--without food. Self-confidence sees the possibilities of the individual; self-reliance realizes them. Self-confidence sees the angel in the unhewn block of marble; self-reliance carves it out for himself.

The man who is self-reliant says ever: "No one can realize my possibilities for me, but me; no one can make me good or evil but myself." He works out his own salvation,--financially, socially, mentally, physically, and morally. Life is an individual problem that man must solve for himself. Nature accepts no vicarious sacrifice, no vicarious service. Nature never recognizes a proxy vote. She has nothing to do with middle-men,--she deals only with the individual. Nature is constantly seeking to show man that he is his own best friend, or his own worst enemy. Nature gives man the option on which he will be to himself.

All the athletic exercises in the world are of no value to the individual unless he compel those bars and dumb-bells to yield to him, in strength and muscle, the power for which he, himself, pays in time and effort. He can never develop his muscles by sending his valet to a gymnasium.

The medicine-chests of the world are powerless, in

all the united efforts, to help the individual until he reach out and take for himself what is needed for his individual weakness.

All the religions of the world are but speculations in morals, mere theories of salvation, until the individual realize that he must save himself by relying on the law of truth, as he sees it, and living his life in harmony with it, as fully as he can. But religion is not a Pullman car, with soft-cushioned seats, where he has but to pay for his ticket,--and some one else does all the rest. In religion, as in all other great things, he is ever thrown back on his self-reliance. He should accept all helps, but,--he must live his own life. He should not feel that he is a mere passenger; he is the engineer, and the train is his life. We must rely on ourselves, live our own lives, or we merely drift through existence,--losing all that is best, all that is greatest, all that is divine.

All that others can do for us is to give us opportunity. We must ever be prepared for the opportunity when it comes, and to go after it and find it when it does not come, or that opportunity is to us,--nothing. Life is but a succession of opportunities. They are for good or evil,-- as we make them.

Many of the alchemists of old felt that they lacked but one element; if they could obtain that one, they believed they could transmute the baser metals into pure gold. It is so in character. There are individuals with rare mental gifts, and delicate spiritual discernment who fail utterly in life because they lack the one element,--self- reliance. This would unite all their energies, and focus them into strength and power.

The man who is not self-reliant is weak, hesitating and doubting in all he does. He fears to take a decisive step, because he dreads failure, because he is waiting for some one to advise him or because he dare not act in accordance with his own best judgment. In his cowardice and his conceit he sees all his non-success due to others. He is "not appreciated," "not recognized," he is "kept down." He feels that in some subtle way "society is conspiring against him." He grows almost vain as he thinks that no one has had such poverty, such sorrow, such affliction, such failure as have come to him.

The man who is self-reliant seeks ever to discover and conquer the weakness within him that keeps him from the attainment of what he holds dearest; he seeks within himself the power to battle against all outside influences. He realizes that all the greatest men in history, in every phase of human effort, have been those who have had to fight against the odds of sickness, suffering, sorrow. To him, defeat is no more than passing through a tunnel is to a traveller,--he knows he must emerge again into the sunlight.

The nation that is strongest is the one that is most self-reliant, the one that contains within its boundaries all that its people need. If, with its ports all blockaded it has not within itself the necessities of life and the elements of its continual progress then,--it is weak, held by the enemy, and it is but a question of time till it must surrender. Its independence is in proportion to its self-reliance, to its power to sustain itself from within. What is true of nations is true of individuals. The history of nations is but the biography of individuals magnified, intensified, multiplied, and projected on the screen of the past. History is the biography of a nation; biography is the history of an individual. So it must be that the individual who is most strong in any trial, sorrow or need is he who can live from his inherent strength, who needs no scaffolding of commonplace sympathy to uphold him. He must ever be self-reliant.

The wealth and prosperity of ancient Rome, relying on her slaves to do the real work of the nation, proved the nation's downfall. The constant dependence on the captives of war to do the thousand details of life for them, killed self-reliance in the nation and in the individual. Then, through weakened self-reliance and the increased opportunity for idle, luxurious ease that came with it, Rome, a nation of fighters, became,--a nation of men more effeminate than women. As we depend on others to do those things we should do for ourselves, our self-reliance weakens and our powers and our control of them becomes continuously less.

Man to be great must be self-reliant. Though he may not be so in all things, he must be self-reliant in the one in which he would be great. This self-reliance is not the self-sufficiency of conceit. It is daring to stand alone. Be an oak, not a vine. Be ready to give support, but do not crave it; do not be dependent on it. To develop your true self- reliance, you must see from the very beginning that life is a battle you must fight for yourself,--you must be your own soldier. You cannot buy a substitute, you cannot win a reprieve, you can never be placed on the retired list. The retired list of life is,--death. The world is busy with its own cares, sorrows and joys, and pays little heed to you. There is but one great password to success,--self-reliance.

If you would learn to converse, put yourself into positions where you *must* speak. If you would conquer your morbidness, mingle with the bright people around you, no matter how difficult it may be. If you desire the power that some one else possesses, do not envy his strength, and dissipate your energy by weakly wishing his force were yours. Emulate the process by which it became his, depend on your self- reliance, pay the price for it, and equal power may be yours. The individual must look upon himself as an investment, of untold possibilities if rightly developed,--a mine whose resources can never be known but by going down into it and bringing out what is hidden.

Man can develop his self-reliance by seeking constantly to surpass himself. We try too much to surpass others. If we seek ever to surpass ourselves, we are moving on a uniform line of progress, that gives a harmonious unifying to our growth in all its parts. Daniel Morrell, at one time President of the Cambria Rail Works, that employed 7,000 men and made a rail famed throughout the world, was asked the secret of the great success of the works. "We have no secret," he said, "but this,-- we always try to beat our last batch of rails." Competition is good, but it has its danger side. There is a tendency to sacrifice real worth to mere appearance, to have seeming rather than reality. But the true competition is the competition of the individual with himself,-- his present seeking to excel his past. This means real growth from within. Self-reliance develops it, and it develops self-reliance. Let the individual feel thus as to his own progress and possibilities, and he can almost create his life as he will. Let him never fall down in despair at dangers and sorrows at a distance; they may be harmless, like Bunyan's stone lions, when he nears them.

The man who is self-reliant does not live in the shadow of some one else's greatness; he thinks for himself, depends on himself, and acts for himself. In throwing the individual thus back upon himself it is not shutting his eyes to the stimulus and light and new life that come with the warm pressure of the hand, the kindly word and the sincere expressions of true friendship. But true friendship is rare; its great value is in a crisis,--like a lifeboat. Many a boasted friend has proved a leaking, worthless "lifeboat" when the storm of adversity might make him useful. In these great crises of life, man is strong only as he is strong from within, and the more he depends on himself the stronger will he become, and the more able will he be to help others in the hour of their need. His very life will be a constant help and a strength to others, as he becomes to them a living lesson of the dignity of self-reliance.

V

Failure as a Success

It ofttimes requires heroic courage to face fruitless effort, to take up the broken strands of a life-work, to look bravely toward the future, and proceed undaunted on our way. But what, to our eyes, may seem hopeless failure is often but the dawning of a greater success. It may contain in its debris the foundation material of a mighty purpose, or the revelation of new and higher possibilities.

Some years ago, it was proposed to send logs from Canada to New York, by a new method. The ingenious plan of Mr. Joggins was to bind great logs together by cables and iron girders and to tow the cargo as a raft. When the novel craft neared New York and success seemed assured, a terrible storm arose. In the fury of the tempest, the iron bands snapped like icicles and the angry waters scattered the logs far and wide. The chief of the Hydrographic Department at Washington heard of the failure of the experiment, and at once sent word to shipmasters the world over, urging them to watch carefully for these logs which he described; and to note the precise location of each in latitude and longitude and the time the observation was made.

Hundreds of captains, sailing over the waters of the earth, noted the logs, in the Atlantic Ocean, in the Mediterranean, in the South Seas-- for into all waters did these venturesome ones travel. Hundreds of reports were made, covering a period of weeks and months. These observations were then carefully collated, systematized and tabulated, and discoveries were made as to the course of ocean currents that otherwise would have been impossible. The loss of the Joggins raft was not a real failure, for it led to one of the great discoveries in modern marine geography and navigation.

In our superior knowledge we are disposed to speak in a patronizing tone of the follies of the alchemists of old. But their failure to transmute the baser metals into gold resulted in the birth of chemistry. They did not succeed in what they attempted, but they brought into vogue the natural processes of sublimation, filtration, distillation, and crystallization; they invented the alembic, the retort, the sand-bath, the water-bath and other valuable instruments. To them is due the discovery of antimony, sulphuric ether and phosphorus, the cupellation of gold and silver, the determining of the properties of saltpetre and its use in gunpowder, and the discovery of the distillation of essential oils. This was the success of failure, a wondrous process of Nature for the highest growth,--a mighty lesson of comfort, strength, and encouragement if man would only realize and accept it.

Many of our failures sweep us to greater heights of success, than we ever hoped for in our wildest dreams. Life is a successive unfolding of success from failure. In discovering America Columbus failed absolutely. His ingenious reasoning and experiment led him to believe that by sailing westward he would reach India. Every redman in

America carries in his name "Indian," the perpetuation of the memory of the failure of Columbus. The Genoese navigator did not reach India; the cargo of "souvenirs" he took back to Spain to show to Ferdinand and Isabella as proofs of his success, really attested his failure. But the discovery of America was a greater success than was any finding of a "back-door" to India.

When David Livingstone had supplemented his theological education by a medical course, he was ready to enter the missionary field. For over three years he had studied tirelessly, with all energies concentrated on one aim,--to spread the gospel in China. The hour came when he was ready to start out with noble enthusiasm for his chosen work, to consecrate himself and his life to his unselfish ambition. Then word came from China that the "opium war" would make it folly to attempt to enter the country. Disappointment and failure did not long daunt him; he offered himself as missionary to Africa,--and he was accepted. His glorious failure to reach China opened a whole continent to light and truth. His study proved an ideal preparation for his labors as physician, explorer, teacher and evangel in the wilds of Africa.

Business reverses and the failure of his partner threw upon the broad shoulders and the still broader honor and honesty of Sir Walter Scott a burden of responsibility that forced him to write. The failure spurred him to almost super-human effort. The masterpieces of Scotch historic fiction that have thrilled, entertained and uplifted millions of his fellow-men are a glorious monument on the field of a seeming failure.

When Millet, the painter of the "Angelus" worked on his almost divine canvas, in which the very air seems pulsing with the regenerating essence of spiritual reverence, he was painting against time, he was antidoting sorrow, he was racing against death. His brush strokes, put on in the early morning hours before going to his menial duties as a railway porter, in the dusk like that perpetuated on his canvas,--meant strength, food and medicine for the dying wife he adored. The art failure that cast him into the depths of poverty unified with marvellous intensity all the finer elements of his nature. This rare spiritual unity, this purging of all the dross of triviality as he passed through the furnace of poverty, trial, and sorrow gave eloquence to his brush and enabled him to paint as never before,--as no prosperity would have made possible.

Failure is often the turning-point, the pivot of circumstance that swings us to higher levels. It may not be financial success, it may not be fame; it may be new draughts of spiritual, moral or mental inspiration that will change us for all the later years of our life. Life is not really what comes to us, but what we get from it.

Whether man has had wealth or poverty, failure or success, counts for little when it is past. There is but one question for him to answer, to face boldly and honestly as an individual alone with his conscience and his destiny:

"How will I let that poverty or wealth affect me? If

that trial or deprivation has left me better, truer, nobler, then,--poverty has been riches, failure has been a success. If wealth has come to me and has made me vain, arrogant, contemptuous, uncharitable, cynical, closing from me all the tenderness of life, all the channels of higher development, of possible good to my fellow-man, making me the mere custodian of a money-bag, then,--wealth has lied to me, it has been failure, not success; it has not been riches, it has been dark, treacherous poverty that stole from me even Myself." All things become for us then what we take from them.

Failure is one of God's educators. It is experience leading man to higher things; it is the revelation of a way, a path hitherto unknown to us. The best men in the world, those who have made the greatest real successes look back with serene happiness on their failures. The turning of the face of Time shows all things in a wondrously illuminated and satisfying perspective.

Many a man is thankful to-day that some petty success for which he once struggled, melted into thin air as his hand sought to clutch it. Failure is often the rock-bottom foundation of real success. If man, in a few instances of his life can say, "Those failures were the best things in the world that could have happened to me," should he not face new failures with undaunted courage and trust that the miraculous ministry of Nature may transform these new stumbling-blocks into new stepping-stones?

Our highest hopes, are often destroyed to prepare us

for better things. The failure of the caterpillar is the birth of the butterfly; the passing of the bud is the becoming of the rose; the death or destruction of the seed is the prelude to its resurrection as wheat. It is at night, in the darkest hours, those preceding dawn, that plants grow best, that they most increase in size. May this not be one of Nature's gentle showings to man of the times when he grows best, of the darkness of failure that is evolving into the sunlight of success. Let us fear only the failure of not living the right as we see it, leaving the results to the guardianship of the Infinite.

If we think of any supreme moment of our lives, any great success, any one who is dear to us, and then consider how we reached that moment, that success, that friend, we will be surprised and strengthened by the revelation. As we trace each one, back, step by step, through the genealogy of circumstances, we will see how logical has been the course of our joy and success, from sorrow and failure, and that what gives us most happiness to-day is inextricably connected with what once caused us sorrow. Many of the rivers of our greatest prosperity and growth have had their source and their trickling increase into volume among the dark, gloomy recesses of our failure.

There is no honest and true work, carried along with constant and sincere purpose that ever really fails. If it sometime seem to be wasted effort, it will prove to us a new lesson of "how" to walk; the secret of our failures will prove to us the inspiration of possible successes. Man living with the highest aims, ever as best he can, in continuous harmony

with them, is a success, no matter what statistics of
failure a near-sighted and half-blind world of critics
and commentators may lay at his door.

High ideals, noble efforts will make seeming
failures but trifles, they need not dishearten us; they
should prove sources of new strength. The rocky
way may prove safer than the slippery path of
smoothness. Birds cannot fly best with the wind but
against it; ships do not progress in calm, when the
sails flap idly against the unstrained masts.

The alchemy of Nature, superior to that of the
Paracelsians, constantly transmutes the baser metals
of failure into the later pure gold of higher success,
if the mind of the worker be kept true, constant and
untiring in the service, and he have that sublime
courage that defies fate to its worst while he does
his best.

VI

Doing Our Best at All Times

Life is a wondrously complex problem for the
individual, until, some day, in a moment of
illumination, he awakens to the great realization
that he can make it simple,--never quite simple, but
always simpler. There are a thousand mysteries of
right and wrong that have baffled the wise men of

the ages. There are depths in the great fundamental questions of the human race that no plummet of philosophy has ever sounded. There are wild cries of honest hunger for truth that seek to pierce the silence beyond the grave, but to them ever echo back,--only a repetition of their unanswered cries.

To us all, comes, at times, the great note of questioning despair that darkens our horizon and paralyzes our effort: "If there really be a God, if eternal justice really rule the world," we say, "why should life be as it is? Why do some men starve while others feast; why does virtue often languish in the shadow while vice triumphs in the sunshine; why does failure so often dog the footsteps of honest effort, while the success that comes from trickery and dishonor is greeted with the world's applause? How is it that the loving father of one family is taken by death, while the worthless incumbrance of another is spared? Why is there so much unnecessary pain, sorrowing and suffering in the world--why, indeed, should there be any?"

Neither philosophy nor religion can give any final satisfactory answer that is capable of logical demonstration, of absolute proof. There is ever, even after the best explanations, a residuum of the unexplained. We must then fall back in the eternal arms of faith, and be wise enough to say, "I will not be disconcerted by these problems of life, I will not permit them to plunge me into doubt, and to cloud my life with vagueness and uncertainty. Man arrogates much to himself when he demands from the Infinite the full solution of all His mysteries. I will found my life on the impregnable rock of a

simple fundamental truth:--'This glorious creation
with its millions of wondrous phenomena pulsing
ever in harmony with eternal law must have a
Creator, that Creator must be omniscient and
omnipotent. But that Creator Himself cannot, in
justice, demand of any creature more than the best
that that individual can give.' I will do each day, in
every moment, the best I can by the light I have; I
will ever seek more light, more perfect illumination
of truth, and ever live as best I can in harmony with
the truth as I see it. If failure come I will meet it
bravely; if my pathway then lie in the shadow of
trial, sorrow and suffering, I shall have the restful
peace and the calm strength of one who has done
his best, who can look back upon the past with no
pang of regret, and who has heroic courage in
facing the results, whatever they be, knowing that
he could not make them different."

Upon this life-plan, this foundation, man may erect
any superstructure of religion or philosophy that he
conscientiously can erect; he should add to his
equipment for living every shred of strength and
inspiration, moral, mental or spiritual that is in his
power to secure. This simple working faith is
opposed to no creed, is a substitute for none; it is
but a primary belief, a citadel, a refuge where the
individual can retire for strength when the battle of
life grows hard.

A mere theory of life, that remains but a theory, is
about as useful to a man, as a gilt-edged menu is to
a starving sailor on a raft in mid- ocean. It is
irritating but not stimulating. No rule for higher
living will help a man in the slightest, until he reach

out and appropriate it for himself, until he make it practical in his daily life, until that seed of theory in his mind blossom into a thousand flowers of thought and word and act.

If a man honestly seeks to live his best at all times, that determination is visible in every moment of his living, no trifle in his life can be too insignificant to reflect his principle of living. The sun illuminates and beautifies a fallen leaf by the roadside as impartially as a towering mountain peak in the Alps. Every drop of water in the ocean is an epitome of the chemistry of the whole ocean; every drop is subject to precisely the same laws as dominate the united infinity of billions of drops that make that miracle of Nature, men call the Sea. No matter how humble the calling of the individual, how uninteresting and dull the round of his duties, he should do his best. He should dignify what he is doing by the mind he puts into it, he should vitalize what little he has of power or energy or ability or opportunity, in order to prepare himself to be equal to higher privileges when they come. This will never lead man to that weak content that is satisfied with whatever falls to his lot. It will rather fill his mind with that divine discontent that cheerfully accepts the best,--merely as a temporary substitute for something better.

The man who is seeking ever to do his best is the man who is keen, active, wide-awake, and aggressive. He is ever watchful of himself in trifles; his standard is not "What will the world say?" but "Is it worthy of me?"

Edwin Booth, one of the greatest actors on the American stage, would never permit himself to assume an ungraceful attitude, even in his hours of privacy. In this simple thing, he ever lived his best. On the stage every move was one of unconscious grace. Those of his company who were conscious of their motions were the awkward ones, who were seeking in public to undo or to conceal the carelessness of the gestures and motions of their private life. The man who is slipshod and thoughtless in his daily speech, whose vocabulary is a collection of anaemic commonplaces, whose repetitions of phrases and extravagance of interjections act but as feeble disguises to his lack of ideas, will never be brilliant on an occasion when he longs to outshine the stars. Living at one's best is constant preparation for instant use. It can never make one over-precise, self-conscious, affected, or priggish. Education, in its highest sense, is *conscious* training of mind or body to act *unconsciously*. It is conscious formation of mental habits, not mere acquisition of information.

One of the many ways in which the individual unwisely eclipses himself, is in his worship of the fetich of luck. He feels that all others are lucky, and that whatever he attempts, fails. He does not realize the untiring energy, the unremitting concentration, the heroic courage, the sublime patience that is the secret of some men's success. Their "luck" was that they had prepared themselves to be equal to their opportunity when it came and were awake to recognize it and receive it. His own opportunity came and departed unnoted, it would not waken him from his dreams of some untold wealth that would fall into his lap. So he grows discouraged and envies those whom he should emulate, and he bandages his arm and chloroforms his energies, and performs his duties in a perfunctory way, or he passes through life, just ever "sampling" lines of activity.

The honest, faithful struggler should always realize that failure is but an episode in a true man's life,-- never the whole story. It is never easy to meet, and no philosophy can make it so, but the steadfast courage to master conditions, instead of complaining of them, will help him on his way; it will ever enable him to get the best out of what he has. He never knows the long series of vanquished failures that give solidity to some one else's success; he does not realize the price that some rich man, the innocent football of political malcontents and demagogues, has heroicly paid for wealth and position.

The man who has a pessimist's doubt of all things; who demands a certified guarantee of his future; who ever fears his work will not be recognized or appreciated; or that after all, it is really not worth while, will never live his best. He is dulling his capacity for real progress by his hypnotic course of excuses for inactivity, instead of a strong tonic of reasons for action.

One of the most weakening elements in the individual make-up is the surrender to the oncoming of years. Man's self-confidence dims and dies in the fear of age. "This new thought," he says of some suggestion tending to higher development, "is good;

it is what we need. I am glad to have it for my children; I would have been happy to have had some such help when I was at school, but it is too late for me. I am a man advanced in years."

This is but blind closing of life to wondrous possibilities. The knell of lost opportunity is never tolled in this life. It is never too late to recognize truth and to live by it. It requires only greater effort, closer attention, deeper consecration; but the impossible does not exist for the man who is self-confident and is willing to pay the price in time and struggle for his success or development. Later in life, the assessments are heavier in progress, as in life insurance, but that matters not to that mighty self-confidence that *will* not grow old while knowledge can keep it young.

Socrates, when his hair whitened with the snow of age, learned to play on instruments of music. Cato, at fourscore, began his study of Greek, and the same age saw Plutarch beginning, with the enthusiasm of a boy, his first lessons in Latin. The Character of Man, Theophrastus' greatest work, was begun on his ninetieth birthday. Chaucer's Canterbury Tales was the work of the poet's declining years. Ronsard, the father of French poetry, whose sonnets even translation cannot destroy, did not develop his poetic faculty until nearly fifty. Benjamin Franklin at this age had just taken his really first steps of importance in philosophic pursuits. Arnauld, the theologian and sage, translated Josephus in his eightieth year. Winckelmann, one of the most famous writers on classic antiquities, was the son of a shoemaker, and lived in obscurity and ignorance until the prime of life. Hobbes, the English philosopher, published his version of the Odyssey in his eighty-seventh year, and his Iliad one year later. Chevreul, the great French scientist, whose untiring labors in the realm of color have so enriched the world, was busy, keen and active when Death called him, at the age of 103.

These men did not fear age; these few names from the great muster-roll of the famous ones who defied the years, should be voices of hope and heartening to every individual whose courage and confidence is weak. The path of truth, higher living, truer development in every phase of life, is never shut from the individual--until he closes it himself. Let man feel this, believe it and make this faith a real and living factor in his life and there are no limits to his progress. He has but to live his best at all times, and rest calm and untroubled no matter what results come to his efforts. The constant looking backward to what might have been, instead of forward to what may be, is a great weakener of self-confidence. This worry for the old past, this wasted energy, for that which no power in the world can restore, ever lessens the individual's faith in himself, weakens his efforts to develop himself for the future to the perfection of his possibilities.

Nature in her beautiful love and tenderness, says to man, weakened and worn and weary with the struggle, "Do in the best way you can the trifle that is under your hand at this moment; do it in the best spirit of preparation for the future your thought suggests; bring all the light of knowledge from all the past to aid you. Do this and you have done your best. The past is forever closed to you. It is closed forever to you. No worry, no struggle, no suffering, no agony of despair can alter it. It is as much beyond your power as if it were a million years of eternity behind you. Turn all that past, with its sad hours, weakness and sin, its wasted opportunities as light; in confidence and hope, upon the future. Turn it all in fuller truth and light so as to make each trifle of this present a new past it will be joy to look back to; each trifle a grander, nobler, and more perfect preparation for the future. The present and the future you can make from it, is yours; the past has gone back, with all its messages, all its history, all its records to the God who loaned you the golden moments to use in obedience to His law."

VII

The Royal Road to Happiness

"During my whole life I have not had twenty-four hours of happiness." So said Prince Bismarck, one of the greatest statesmen of the nineteenth century. Eighty-three years of wealth, fame, honors, power, influence, prosperity and triumph,--years when he held an empire in his fingers,-- but not one day of happiness!

Happiness is the greatest paradox in Nature. It can grow in any soil, live under any conditions. It defies environment. It comes from within; it is the revelation of the depths of the inner life as light and heat proclaim the sun from which they radiate. Happiness consists not of having, but of being; not of possessing, but of enjoying. It is the warm glow of a heart at peace with itself. A martyr at the stake may have happiness that a king on his throne might envy. Man is the creator of his own happiness; it is the aroma of a life lived in harmony with high ideals. For what a man *has*, he may be dependent on others; what he *is*, rests with him alone. What he *ob*tains in life is but acquisition; what he *at*tains, is growth. Happiness is the soul's joy in the possession of the intangible. Absolute, perfect, continuous happiness in life, is impossible for the human. It would mean the consummation of attainments, the individual consciousness of a perfectly fulfilled destiny. Happiness is paradoxic because it may coexist with trial, sorrow and poverty. It is the gladness of the heart,--rising superior to all conditions.

Happiness has a number of under-studies,-- gratification, satisfaction, content, and pleasure,-- clever imitators that simulate its appearance rather than emulate its method. Gratification is a harmony between our desires and our possessions. It is ever incomplete, it is the thankful acceptance of part. It is a mental pleasure in the quality of what one receives, an unsatisfiedness as to the quantity. It may be an element in happiness, but, in itself,--it is not happiness.

Satisfaction is perfect identity of our desires and our possessions. It exists only so long as this perfect union and unity can be preserved. But every realized ideal gives birth to new ideals, every step in advance reveals large domains of the unattained; every feeding stimulates new appetites,--then the desires and possessions are no longer identical, no longer equal; new cravings call forth new activities, the equipoise is destroyed, and dissatisfaction reenters. Man might possess everything tangible in the world and yet not be happy, for happiness is the satisfying of the soul, not of the mind or the body. Dissatisfaction, in its highest sense, is the keynote of all advance, the evidence of new aspirations, the guarantee of the progressive revelation of new possibilities.

Content is a greatly overrated virtue. It is a kind of diluted despair; it is the feeling with which we continue to accept substitutes, without striving for the realities. Content makes the trained individual swallow vinegar and try to smack his lips as if it were wine. Content enables one to warm his hands at the fire of a past joy that exists only in memory. Content is a mental and moral chloroform that deadens the activities of the individual to rise to higher planes of life and growth. Man should never be contented with anything less than the best efforts of his nature can possibly secure for him. Content makes the world more comfortable for the individual, but it is the death-knell of progress. Man should be content with each step of progress merely as a station, discontented with it as a destination; contented with it as a step; discontented with it as a finality. There are times when a man should be content with what he *has*, but never with what he *is*.

But content is not happiness; neither is pleasure. Pleasure is temporary, happiness is continuous; pleasure is a note, happiness is a symphony; pleasure may exist when conscience utters protests; happiness,--never. Pleasure may have its dregs and its lees; but none can be found in the cup of happiness.

Man is the only animal that can be really happy. To the rest of the creation belong only weak imitations of the understudies. Happiness represents a peaceful attunement of a life with a standard of living. It can never be made by the individual, by himself, for himself. It is one of the incidental by-products of an unselfish life. No man can make his own happiness the one object of his life and attain it, any more than he can jump on the far end of his shadow. If you would hit the bull's-eye of happiness on the target of life, aim above it. Place other things higher than your own happiness and it will surely come to you. You can buy pleasure, you can acquire content, you can become satisfied,--but Nature never put real happiness on the bargain-counter. It is the undetachable accompaniment of true living. It is calm and peaceful; it never lives in an atmosphere of worry or of hopeless struggle.

The basis of happiness is the love of something outside self. Search every instance of happiness in the world, and you will find, when all the incidental features are eliminated, there is always the constant, unchangeable element of love,--love of parent for child; love of man and woman for each other; love of humanity in some form, or a great life work into which the individual throws all his energies.

Happiness is the voice of optimism, of faith, of simple, steadfast love. No cynic or pessimist can be really happy. A cynic is a man who is morally near-sighted,--and brags about it. He sees the evil in his own heart, and thinks he sees the world. He lets a mote in his eye eclipse the sun. An incurable cynic is an individual who should long for death,--for life cannot bring him happiness, death might. The keynote of Bismarck's lack of happiness was his profound distrust of human nature.

There is a royal road to happiness; it lies in Consecration, Concentration, Conquest and Conscience.

Consecration is dedicating the individual life to the service of others, to some noble mission, to realizing some unselfish ideal. Life is not something to be lived *through*; it is something to be lived *up to*. It is a privilege, not a penal servitude of so many decades on earth. Consecration places the object of life above the mere acquisition of money, as a finality. The man who is unselfish, kind, loving, tender, helpful, ready to lighten the burden of those around him, to hearten the struggling ones, to forget himself sometimes in remembering others,--is on the right road to happiness. Consecration is ever active, bold and aggressive, fearing naught but possible disloyalty to high ideals.

Concentration makes the individual life simpler and deeper. It cuts away the shams and pretences of modern living and limits life to its truest essentials. Worry, fear, useless regret,--all the great wastes that sap mental, moral or physical energy must be sacrificed, or the individual needlessly destroys half the possibilities of living. A great purpose in life, something that unifies the strands and threads of each day's thinking, something that takes the sting from the petty trials, sorrows, sufferings and blunders of life, is a great aid to Concentration. Soldiers in battle may forget their wounds, or even be unconscious of them, in the inspiration of battling for what they believe is right. Concentration dignifies an humble life; it makes a great life,--sublime. In morals it is a short-cut to simplicity. It leads to right for right's sake, without thought of policy or of reward. It brings calm and rest to the individual,--a serenity that is but the sunlight of happiness.

Conquest is the overcoming of an evil habit, the rising superior to opposition and attack, the spiritual exaltation that comes from resisting the invasion of the grovelling material side of life. Sometimes when you are worn and weak with the struggle; when it seems that justice is a dream, that honesty and loyalty and truth count for nothing, that the devil is the only good paymaster; when hope grows dim and flickers, then is the time when you must tower in the great sublime faith that Right must prevail, then must you throttle these imps of doubt and despair, you must master yourself to master the world around you. This is Conquest; this is what counts. Even a log can float with the current, it takes a man to fight sturdily against an opposing tide that would sweep his craft out of its course. When the jealousies, the petty intrigues and the meannesses and the misunderstandings in life assail you,--rise above them. Be like a lighthouse that illumines and beautifies the snarling, swashing waves of the storm that threaten it, that seek to undermine it and seek to wash over it. This is Conquest. When the chance to win fame, wealth, success or the attainment of your heart's desire, by sacrifice of honor or principle, comes to you and it does not affect you long enough even to seem a temptation, you have been the victor. That too is Conquest. And Conquest is part of the royal road to Happiness.

Conscience, as the mentor, the guide and compass of every act, leads ever to Happiness. When the individual can stay alone with his conscience and get its approval, without using force or specious logic, then he begins to know what real Happiness is. But the individual must be careful that he is not appealing to a conscience perverted or deadened by the wrongdoing and subsequent deafness of its owner. The man who is honestly seeking to live his life in Consecration, Concentration and Conquest, living from day to day as best he can, by the light he has, may rely explicitly on his Conscience. He can shut his ears to "what the world says" and find in the approval of his own conscience the highest earthly tribune,--the voice of the Infinite communing with the Individual.

Unhappiness is the hunger to get; Happiness is the hunger to give. True happiness must ever have the tinge of sorrow outlived, the sense of pain softened by the mellowing years, the chastening of loss that in the wondrous mystery of time transmutes our suffering into love and sympathy with others.

If the individual should set out for a single day to give Happiness, to make life happier, brighter and sweeter, not for himself, but for others, he would find a wondrous revelation of what Happiness really is. The greatest of the world's heroes could not by any series of acts of heroism do as much real good as any individual living his whole life in seeking, from day to day, to make others happy.

Each day there should be fresh resolution, new strength, and renewed enthusiasm. "Just for Today" might be the daily motto of thousands of societies throughout the country, composed of members bound together to make the world better through constant simple acts of kindness, constant deeds of sweetness and love. And Happiness would come to them, in its highest and best form, not because they would seek to *absorb* it, but,--because they seek to *radiate* it.

Made in the USA
San Bernardino, CA
02 December 2016